When They Can't Relate

Norma McLucas

My Experiences, From my Heart, Through my
Pen.

Editor: Lois E. Love

This book is dedicated to:

Everyone in the workforce or retired who has experienced adversities in the workplace, and could not have their voices heard or their issues addressed.

Acknowledgements:

My sincere thanks to The Creator, for everything, also to my daughter, Dawn McLucas, and my mentor, Joy E. Mason, for their assistance, encouragement, and motivation. Last but not least, special thanks to my husband, Vincent McLucas, for being there, caring, and for giving me his professional advice, as well as listening to me vent.

ISBN 979-8-9875030-6-5 PBK

March 2023

BluePrint Ambitions

blueprintambitions.com

Indianapolis, IN

Table of Contents

Chapter 1: The Journey

In order to create an accurate reenactment of my journey from the beginning to my retirement, we are going to have to go way back in time. It was 1965 and I was young and fresh out of high school. I was eager to join the workforce. God blessed me with a good job as an assembler at Western Electric. My mother had instilled in me the importance of having a good work ethic and how the game was played. Like most people in the workforce, my top priorities were money and position. Little did I know before my journey ended, I would be in the fight of my life to protect and maintain my individuality, self-confidence, self-esteem, and to ensure that my spirit remained intact.

After twelve years, due to Affirmative Action in March of 1977, I was promoted to the position of supervisor. I did not have any leadership experience or knowledge, and very few willing mentors. It was common knowledge that I was a token supervisor, but I was determined to be the best I could be. After five years in supervision, we were told the plant was being closed and we could relocate or be separated from the company. By this time, I was married and had been blessed with my only daughter. Relocation was not an option for me. My stress level was through the roof. In 1985, I was once again searching for a job. I was too old to be young and too young to be old.

They say when one door closes another one will open. With faith and determination, it is true. In 1987, God blessed me with my final job. Like my first job it also was a good job. My top priority was to be there until I retired. The first six years were good. I was told and I believed the sky was the limit. The seventh year I discovered the sky was obstructed by the cloudy, distorted glass ceiling. Through my experiences, I had acquired some good people skills, production knowledge, a sense of fair play, and a unique management/employee prospective.

When the opportunity presented itself, I decided to train for and assume a leadership role. This was when the character assassinations started. They continued for six years. Management could not relate and stood on the sidelines, until God intervened. They took their toll, but through the grace of God, I survived. I retired in 2009. I was a Production Technician when I hired in and I was a Production Technician when I left. I had the ability, put forth the effort, and I had acquired the knowledge and skills to advance. My qualifications were constantly on display and documented. Advancement or not, I was a winner, because when I retired, excluding age, I was basically the same person that I was when I hired in. Let the games continue, because the beat goes on.

Chapter 2: Snapshots

(Conversations with co-workers)

Comment: "You need to change your personality. That is why they don't like you."

Answer: I was born with my personality. It is permanent. You can change behaviors and adjust attitudes, but not personalities. I said brother man please, you deal with them your way and I will deal with them mine.

Comment: "I respect the way you do your job, but I do not respect you as a person."

Answer: I respect everyone and everyone's right to be who they are and to think and feel the way they do. The relationship we had is over. From this day forward, our relationship will be strictly a business one.

Comment: "I will have to remain neutral."

Answer: I understand. You do not want any drama. It is not easy being me. I do not take it personally.

(Conversations with my supervisor)

Comment: "You can't win."

Answer: I am a winner! They have taken money out of my pocket, ruined my good reputation, and labeled me a troublemaker. I have tried not to fight, I do not want to fight, but I know how to fight. I have not lived a sheltered life and I do not need anyone to run interference for me. They are coming after me. Now, I will fight to protect and maintain my individuality, self-esteem, self- confidence, and my spirit, in other words, my right to be me.

Comment: "You need to work on some of the areas for improvement stated on your peer feedback sheets."

Answer: I have addressed one point that I felt was valid. All the other points are personal. They do not address what I do or how I perform my duties. They are directed at who I am so therefore they are invalid.

Comment: "We are all friends in this department except for you."

Answer: I will be as friendly as they will let me, or as distant as they make me. We are not friends. Is it a requirement that we be friends to work in this department? Is this a social club or a business? I am so confused.

(Conversations with manager)

Comment: "I do not think that you are giving your friend enough credit for their friendship."

Answer: Some people use the term friend too loosely. Friends respect, trust, socialize, and care about each other. On my job, I have some good and some indifferent associates. I do not have any true friends at work.

Comment: "Your personality is unsuitable for a leadership role."

Answer: That is not what your Diversity Policy states. Personal style and personality are acceptable differences. Are you saying that I can't be me and get paid for what I do and how I do it?

Comment: "Your peers feel intimidated by you. You control the environment and have a negative effect on the department."

Answer: If I had the power to control the work environment, it would be a positive one, unlike the current negative one that exists today. I am not the one controlling the environment.

(Conversations with Human Resources)

Comment: "You are going to have to deal with your peers on a different level."

Answer: I am already on a different level. I am up here and they are down there clawing, digging, and hating.

Comment: " You are so strong, they don't think that they are getting to you."

Answer: Is that why we are here? Yes, thank God and my mother for my strength, but even iron wears out under constant pressure.

Comment: "Some of your co-workers who share your culture have made negative comments about you."

Answer: Do you think that we all like each other? Surprise, we don't.

Comment: "Can you just give them what they are used to?"

Answer: No, I cannot and will not give them what they are used to, because that is the problem. They have been doing wrong so long that they think they are right. They need to be challenged.

Chapter 3: Momma Used to Say

Don't play with me.

      When I was around eight years of age, I raised my hand to my mother. I heard her say," no child of mine is going to raise their hand to me." I guess the Devil made me do it. My mother had something for both of us. I do not remember getting hit, or the pain associated with the action. All I remember, is that I was sliding at a high rate of speed across the kitchen floor. I don't have any idea which way the Devil went, but when I stopped sliding, I was under the kitchen sink peeping out of the curtain around the bottom. My right hand was still up in the air. I waited until the coast was clear to make my exit, stage left through the back kitchen door. The Devil got me hurt and he could have got me killed. Never again, did I let him convince me to disrespect my mother.

Food for thought-----We all have a little negative voice in our heads. Listening to it is not a good or healthy practice. (why I ought to) That little voice could get us hurt or killed. We cannot turn it off, but we can and should tune it out.

My older brother and sister were fighters. One day they were in the backyard fighting each other. He was socking it to her good. I ran and told my mother and then I watched from a safe distance. My brother's mind must have snapped, because when my mother broke up the fight, he picked up a brick. My mother asked him what he was going to do with that brick. His mind must have returned, because his answer was "what brick?" He dropped the brick and took off running. My mother said in a calm voice "you can run, but you will have to come back and I will be here waiting on you." He knew that he was going to get it because our mother did not lie or threaten. She made promises and she always kept them.

Food for thought----you can run, but if you do something wrong sooner or later you will have to face the consequences.

Yo momma

My older brother and sister loved to fight and they were good at it. Not me, I had a chicken heart and Road Runner legs. I'm out of here. Catch me if you can. (beep – beep) One day they both came home all beat up. My mother took one look at them and knew they had been fighting again. She asked them what the fight was about. They told her someone was talking about her. She asked them what they said. They said yo momma. That was the number one fight phrase. She smiled and asked, "Do they know me?" They said no. She replied, "So you both got beat up for nothing." She told them to get out of her face, and to go somewhere and sit down. She told them to pick their fights, because sometimes it is better to say, "there they go than there they lay."

Bad days

My mother told me I would have some bad days, but not even my mother could have thought or believed that the bad days would last for six years. I am thankful she gave me a survival kit with all the tools that I need. (pray, have faith, wait, and endure)

Chapter 4: Personally Speaking

1. The words we choose and the tone we use may determine how others receive and respond to what we have to say.
2. There is only one race of people. God created the Human Race, and the people are multicultural and multicolored.
3. A group of individuals think independently, while cliques surrender their individuality and think collectively.
4. When people size us up, there is very little that we can do to convince them that the method they are using is outdated or defective.
5. When all else fails---- pray harder and more often, Prayer Works. Let go and let God.
6. Some people fail to see us as we really are, it may be because they are looking at us through the eyes of others. (They are under the influence).
7. When your best efforts are not acknowledged, do not be discouraged. Take pride in and celebrate your accomplishments. (Occasionally, it is acceptable to pat ourselves on the back).
8. Pretenders will say and do whatever they feel is necessary in order to fake their way to the top.
9. Everyday people are consistently and exactly who they appear to be, they are for real.
10. Laughter is healthy and very therapeutic. Making fun of others is the exception.
11. Unprofessional, unqualified, weak, or bad managers give a good business a bad name.

Chapter 5: Summary

When individuals enter the workforce, they should set flexible priorities and realistic goals. They should be conscious of the fact that in life everything constantly changes and that they will have to regroup and adapt to changes. Individuals should prepare and set attainable goals and boundaries. They should decide how they define success and the path they need to take to achieve it. "To thine own self be true."

From my perspective, there are four phases of life. Phase one is childhood, phase two is young adulthood, phase three is middle age, and phase four is old age. I am in phase four. Writing and publishing this book has helped me to put phase three in the past and to live and enjoy the final phase. Unfortunately, my story is not unique, but it is just extremely personal. God is good and may the game of life continue.

THE END

AND

THE BEGINNING

About the Author

The authors' purpose for writing and publishing this book is to add some information and insight into her thoughts written in her first book. She also hopes that her readers will enjoy and be encouraged by the contents of this book.

www.ingramcontent.com/pod-product-compliance
Lightning Source LLC
Chambersburg PA
CBHW040821150626
46551CB00038BA/1675